Psalms of the Dining Room

Emily,
"Poetry, like bread,
is for everyone"
Thank you!
Warmly,
Swannie

Psalms of the Dining Room

LAUREN SCHMIDT

WIPF & STOCK · Eugene, Oregon

PSALMS OF THE DINING ROOM

Wipf & Stock
An Imprint of Wipf and Stock Publishers
199 W. 8th Ave., Suite 3
Eugene, OR 97401
www.wipfandstock.com

ISBN 13: 978-1-61097-427-1

Manufactured in the U.S.A.

To Josie,
For imagining The Dining Room

Contents

Foreword

THE POETRY of Lauren Schmidt does what poetry should do: make the invisible visible, indelibly, unforgettably. If ever a collection of poems embodied Whitman's dictum to speak for "the rights of them the others are down upon," this is it.

The poet worked for several years as a volunteer at The Dining Room in Eugene, Oregon, a free meals program (what used to be called a "soup kitchen") sponsored by Food for Lane County. Their motto was "Dining With Dignity," and indeed those who dined there—the poor, the unemployed, the physically and mentally disabled, veterans, the homeless—suffer from an acute, and sometimes lethal, deprivation of dignity in their daily lives.

The poems inspired by the experience of working with this community—in The Dining Room and beyond—humanize the dehumanized, compelling us to see what we do not see and hear what we do not hear, to gaze upon the "ugly" until it becomes beautiful, to re-imagine, re-invent and repair the world.

These are poems of lament, praise, and thanksgiving; thus, they are truly psalms, and belong to that Biblical tradition. They also belong to the tradition of poets who have rolled up their sleeves to work to among the damned, and have written from that perspective. Think of Whitman, laboring in the Civil War hospitals of Washington, D.C., and his poem, "The Wound-Dresser;" or Theodore Deppe, employed as a psychiatric nurse working with adolescents in Willimantic, Connecticut, and his poem, "Admission, Children's Unit," or Rafael Campo, a doctor in the emergency rooms of Boston, and his sonnet cycle, "Ten Patients and Another."

According to *The Eugene Weekly*, on the winter evening of January 25th, 2007, a survey of the homeless counted 2,296 souls in the shelters and on the streets of that city. The number is an abstraction, easily skipped by the mind's eye; the poet must translate that abstraction into something tangibly human. The collective voice of the homeless rises from the gutter in, "The Men Who Grow From Curbs":

> Our spines are made of streetlights.
> We sweat a stew of soot and grease.
> Our Labradors starve in leaves.
> We are the keepers of forgotten things:
> coffee mugs from Christmas, Rudolph's
> shiny head, handle made of antlers.
> The Marilyn Monroe candlestick.
> The Yosemite bison magnet.
> The badminton racket bent like a busted nose.

The poem remembers, in jeweled detail, "the keepers of forgotten things," themselves forgotten. Treated like trash, they treat the trash like gold.

The poet does not impose the artificial light of dignity on the subject; rather, she finds the natural light of dignity within the subject, the luminosity of even the most wounded faces. Beneath the Jefferson Street Bridge in Eugene, we have this scene as rendered with delicate brush strokes of language in the poem, "One Week After Christmas":

> On a patch of grass, once green,
> beneath an overpass of sky,
> off a ramp of Interstate 105,
> three men steady a tree. Dead
> at its ends, branches angled
> from rest on the side of the road
> where it was discovered, then dragged
> here to stand . . .

This ceremony subverts our expectations, stripping the Christmas scene of the usual mercantile sentimentality, demonstrating that human beings can create a home—and meaningful rituals—anywhere:

> . . . Not
> kids sleighing, mouths open
> in glee; not mothers baking,
> fathers praying near a manger;
> not a snowman; not a choo-choo train;
> but three men standing back
> to admire their tree: its branches
> looped with Caution tape,
> foil fangled for its star.

A series of poems addresses the murder of a homeless man, Herbert "Pac-Man" Bishop, a patron of The Dining Room. "As I Roll Silverware" is dedicated to Bishop, who was beaten and left to die with twenty-three separate rib fractures:

> there beneath the Jefferson Street Bridge,
> where he lived, beneath the Jefferson Street Bridge,
> trying to sleep beneath the bridge.

The poem recalls the names of the other nameless ones who pass through The Dining Room every day, too many of them as endangered as Herbert Bishop. There is a refrain that keeps the beat of lamentation and remembrance, based on the rhythm of rolling the silverware for the evening meal:

> Wrap. Roll. Stack it.
> Wrap. Roll. Stack it . . .
>
> In the quietest hour, before the first meal is served,
> I bundle the evening's silverware,
> and practice all their names.

Yet there are also hymns of celebration. "Far from Butter" praises, in language both tactile and lyrical at once, the labor that goes into the creation of an everyday object. That labor and its final product are not only unappreciated, but sacred, as this striking passage makes clear:

> . . . I don't have the shoulders
> to churn that butter, or the hands to give it its texture.
> It is only in feeling a bar begin to melt beneath
> my warm grip, like a muscle grown weak,
>
> that I realize how far I am from butter, the work
> it takes to make that butter. The kind of work
> that is holy like butter. Not water-into-wine work,
> but real work, hard work, work we can be grateful exists
>
> if for no other reason than the joy that comes
> when it's done. I want to taste that holiness,
> so I pull a pat of nickel-thick butter stuck to the flat edge
> of the blade and drop it on my tongue.

If there are poems in praise of work, there are poems in praise of simple communication as well. The denizens of The Dining Room are sealed off by silence from the wider world; how fitting, then, that "The Milk Rule" captures a moment of perfect communication, without a word being spoken:

> As I reach over
> a man to give him
> one small cup of milk,
> he grabs me
> just above the elbow,
> just below the wrist,
> slips his drug-black gums
> around my forearm.
> A harmless beast
> pretending to eat,
> he snarls at my skin,
> slimes me with a mixture
> of spit and scraps
> of half-chewed,
> broiled meat.

Drawing laughter rather than blood, the beast "howls with delight," breaking through his silence, and the wall that separates him from the rest of society. Some might read this as an example of dining with *indignity*, though any moment of shared humanity, however fleeting, has its grace.

Indeed, there is an abundance of grace and hope in these poems, even where despair would be the expected response. In the poem, "Manny," the poet conjures a world where all things are possible, because something "impossible" has actually occurred:

> Manny got a job today. After nine months
> of pushing peas around his plate, eyes he could not
> bear to lift, Manny got a job today.

Manny could be a character in Eugene O'Neill's *The Iceman Cometh*, burdened by the "pipe dream" of the life he once had, or could have again. Yet, in an in environment as full of human suffering as Harry Hope's saloon, Manny—and the poet—refuse the sedative of despair. Instead, the poem invokes the logic of miracles. If Manny could get a job, then, it follows, this could be:

> . . . the day the fear coiled in Doyle's mind lifts
> like smoke rings and fades, the day he forgets
> his wife's bones he put above a fire. This could be
>
> the day Jay's machine-gun gibberish becomes prayer
> or poetry, praise or warning, the day the tank in his throat
> cranks its belts into the soft pulses of a baritone,
> the day he learns to sing. This could be
>
> the day the scar that halves Marva's face unzips,
> the day her albino eye flushes its gray and glimmers,
> warm with brown and sight again, the day the right side
> of her face sits on the throne of her skull . . .

With this cascade of miraculous images, so vividly imagined, the poet moves from witness to visionary, expressing the sure knowledge that a vision of the impossible, expressed in the language of the possible, must precede any great change, personal or political, intimate or global. By poem's end, she envisions a world, where, paradoxically, The Dining Room goes out of business, not due to government cutbacks or the myopic refusal to raise taxes, but because such "soup kitchens" are no longer necessary. The "silver stays in drawers." This could be:

> The day the doors are boarded up, the day the *Closed* sign is hung.
> Manny got a job today. Yes, Manny got a job today.

Fittingly enough, *Psalms of The Dining Room* ends with a poem called, "Prayer." This is a poem of thanksgiving, thankfully free of any reference to the gluttonous holiday of that name and, once again, a true psalm. Cleaning up tables, the poet discovers a scrap of paper left behind by a patron, promising to pray for her. The first reaction is incredulity: "*Pray* for me? Pray for *me*?"

Using this reaction as a point of departure, the poem takes flight. "Pray for me" becomes an incantatory phrase—the poet has a particular gift for anaphora—and a plea for compassion, not only in the world but within the self:

> . . . Because the first thought of my day
> is hunger, pray for me that I eat. But pray for me that I know
> hunger, pray for me. Pray for me that I feel myself
> in the growl of your belly, that I am more like you
> than I remember, pray for me.

As the poem begins to soar, there is a remarkable synthesis: it speaks in the voice of both the suffering human being and the human being who provides relief from suffering, the compassionate one and the one in need of compassion:

> . . . Pray for me that I am
> the blind man because the room knows to make room for him.
> People move tables, chairs, themselves, part a path for him as if
> he were a king. But pray for me that I make way, pray for me.
>
> (. . .)

> . . . Pray for me that I am
> the pregnant girl who is allowed a second plate. Pray that I know
> the power I hold in my body, for a tiny king can grow eyes
>
> in my body, please pray. Pray for me that I am the man
> in this same room, seated at another table, the man
> that gives the girl his milk. Pray for me that I remember
> to give up my milk. Pray for me that I am the milk.

Here is a solidarity that goes beyond rhetoric. Here is a prayer that even an atheist (like me, or like the poet for that matter) can say out loud, for this prayer directs itself, not at God, but at the best in humanity, and the best in ourselves.

In that spirit, praise the poetry of Lauren Schmidt. Praise the *Psalms of The Dining Room*. Let us be thankful for this clear, strong voice, singing for all of us.

Martín Espada
July 2011

Acknowledgments

Fifth Wednesday Journal

"Unwintering"

Little Patuxent Review.

"One Week After Christmas"

Mayday Magazine

"Urban Legend"
"Gridlock"
"Elimination Half-Life"
"The Men Who Grow from Curbs"

The New Verse News

"The Indication"
"Reasons"
"Under the Blows"
"Pac-Man"
"Justice"
"The Perpetrator's Guide to Thrill Killing:
Lesson One: How to Kill a Kitten"

Nimrod

"What I Learned from Birds"

PANK

"Kenneth's Purse"
"Marlon's Fingers"

The Progressive

"Manny"
"Far From Butter"

Provo Orem Word

"A Prayer"

Ruminate

"The Magic Trick of the Table"

The Splinter Generation

"The Coffee Station"
"Her Name is Sarah"
"The Volunteer"

Several of these poems were included in a chapbook called *The Voodoo Doll Parade* (Main Street Rag Publishing Company).

"What I Learned from Birds" was a semi-finalist for the 2009 Pablo Neruda Prize for Poetry.

Part One

Ask Me

After William Stafford

When graffiti becomes gospel, ask me
if I've ever believed in anything.

When telephone poles carry saviors,
when they conduct the Word, ask me

if I've posted my inky prayers on them. Ask me
if any tabs with my number are missing,
or if I've gotten any calls.

When psalms lift from sewers, ask me
if I've let mine go up in a rising wind,

if I can hear them in the stillness of coming and going
and going again.

Some time, when traffic raises the dead, ask me
if I believe in Heaven, and I'll show you the world

underneath my shoe where we must cover our mouths
from the manic stench of a man who lives there.

His hair clumps into horns at his forehead,
and the wolves of his eyes click corner to corner.

PSALMS OF THE DINING ROOM

Some time, when pedestrians are the faithful, ask me
to hold out my hand for peace. Ask me if anyone

reaches to touch me. Some time, when transients
are the prophets, ask me if I ever read their signs.

When crosswalks are the stations, ask me
to lift my back into the oaken wind, ask me

to follow the bridge of skeletons to the safer side.

And when the stoplight changes green to red, ask me
if I can begin again, if I know to pause for a miracle, ask me,

as I'm almost run over, to follow the blinking light
of a man who seems to know the way. Ask me
if my feet need a bath when I get there.

What this city says, that is what I will say.

Gridlock

A teenage girl in too-high heels stamps past a line of cars.
Held by a stop sign, drivers wait for her
patent leather daggers to pass. Her stagger begins

to slow: she knows they cannot go until she's gone.
She idles in the crosswalk, stages herself before the cars
in a half-deserted plea to be seen. She needs someone to see her

studded belt, her stockings like an electric fence, the tear
that reveals her knee. She needs someone to see her
hood— trimmed in exhaust-gray faux fur— about to drop

over her face. She needs someone to see the gaze
behind those thick black straps of eye-lining wax,
streaks like tire tracks of a garbage truck that motor over her

soft and seamless blue, someone to see the beauty
of her rouge-ruined cheeks. Instead, the cars see her
lips bust up with *Fuck you!* from some mucked up misery,

mixed inside then spewing out. She turns on her toes
with a told-them-so swiftness and off slips her shoe.
In all patent leather tragedy, she snatches the heel and cradles it

to her chest. The child hobbles to the curb she came from
almost not crying. And as the skinny-stitched skirt shimmies
to the brim of her waist, she tugs at it, trying to hide

the tops of her thighs—trying to save what little she knows to save.

Meth Mask

What did she see in the cracked-mirror
compact as she scrunched up her lips
in a slapstick strain of a kiss, as she
cocked her brow in a dim bedroom,
laughed at the charming thing
the mirror said? What did she see
as she fish-sucked her cheeks
to give shadows to her cheekbones,
as she pinched the tip of her nose
in hopes it would stay, fluffed the smoke
and dust of her hair? Did she see
the buttons beneath her skin pop off
into fleshy mouths? Did she see
the sores breathe their glue? Did she see
the veins in her eyes cast a net,
red where the white should be? A mouth
so black, as if gummed with motor oil?
Or was the powder an adequate disguise?

Metallurgy

She opens her shirt the way women do
to have rock stars sign their breasts.

But this is no concert and the cop
on the sidewalk strains to pin her

arms behind her back for a check.
Tremors scatter from her chest,

screams, like locusts', color the sky.
He winces at her rotted, copper breath.

No meth left on her. Her half-shed shirt,
like a label from a tin can, flutters

in the struggle. On these streets,
dignity peels away and lives

are crushed and dumpstered.
But the Tin Man finds his nerve,

or was it his mind he was looking for?
No, the Scarecrow sang

If I Only Had a Brain
and the Lion was a weeper.

The Tin Man pined for a heart,
as if any of these things matter.

PSALMS OF THE DINING ROOM

We fashion ourselves with
what is available (or do we

stuff ourselves with all
that's missing), so we're all

a little Tin Man-plus-Scarecrow
and Dorothy with her ruby shoes.

We're all a little asking *How
did I ever get here?* the poor man's

There's no place like home.
We're all a little waiting

for that first burst of hue, but *Somewhere
over the Rainbow* is only in a soup ad.

And here, the woman crumples
to the ground. She slams her face

into her palms and sobs. The cop car
careens away. The gust of his departure

flings the sleeve of her shirt up
in a shiver. Sirens flicker, but are silent.

Bipedal

A woman, pearled and pink-cardiganed, strides toward the library
with her son. Her *I-am-not-not-trying-to-notice-you* poise
is so well rehearsed, she locks into its costume on a sudden.

She feels about the people who dawdle on the curb
much like she feels about gum on her shoe:
not altogether a huge disruption, but the kind

of inconvenience best handled with a stick
and rubber gloves. She knows she shouldn't be bothered,
say, by the man in a kangaroo suit. It's not like he waves

at children or gives them balloons which might be
a sort of public service, a Pavlovian enticement
parents can use: *If we go to the library you will*

see the Kangaroo! And then pandemonium
and children drooling for books. Never mind
that it's summer and that the fuzzy head is shredded

and half-hanging from the neck. Never mind
the hole in the crotch, or that he holds a soda bottle
like he's taking a piss. The woman wants to

but doesn't stuff her son in her purse and saunter past
her marsupial foil whose joeys grow up on these sidewalks
to say *Good Morning* when it's after three o'clock,

or wear dry-markered t-shirts that read: *I shall not fuck*
a woman who, an abortion, would have not. She forges past

trying not to look like she's trying not to look. This is the best she can do.

And tonight, like every Friday night, her arm lifts
from the cape of her cashmere cardigan with the grandeur
of a queen. She toasts her party with a martini and a joke:

A priest, a politician, and a kangaroo walk into a bar . . .

all the while, a leaf of basil is trapped in her veneers.
Her guests are too polite to tell her, but not too polite
to stare—just enough to not-not notice and continue
conversation.

So when she goes into the bathroom before bed, she sees it:
the verdant horror of it all. She paces the tiles trying to clock
the moment she ate the hors d'oeuvre, estimating

how many people over the course of the evening
must have noticed, wondering how many times
they had to look away just to stand to look at her at all.

Seasonally Affected

If this weather had a condition, there'd be a pill for it,

a name to prescribe it, derived from the Latin
twice and then, *marked by extremes.*

If this weather had a personality, it would have many:

a child punching his head in tantrums of rain;
a wallflower lowering her face in the arc of a drink;
a Clint Eastwood kind of wind.

If this weather had a voice, it would talk to itself

in different registers, decibels and genders. It would howl
at its echo, chase its tail around an early moon,
sing sirens to a grease fire.

If this weather had a face, it would glimmer
in the convex grin of a spoon.

If this weather had hair, it would be in the soup:

a lone straggler people pull from their lips, repulsed by
and innately suspicious of.

Water drowns the ankles where the sidewalk meets the street.
As leaves collect in the sewer grates of 8th Avenue,
a homeless man chews calluses from his feet,
then spits them like sunflower seeds.

If this weather had a foot, it would be gnawing at its toe.

The Men Who Grow from Curbs

We're made of beer cans and cardboard.
We crease in November wind.
Our blood streams in the whiz of cars.
We groan like engines, wear mismatched boots.
Our eyes are gears that crank a screen
of all the lives we'll never live to see.
Our skin is yesterday's *New York Times*.
Our spines are made of streetlights.
We sweat a stew of soot and grease.
Our Labradors starve in leaves.
We are the keepers of forgotten things:
coffee mugs from Christmas, Rudolph's
shiny head, handle made of antlers.
The Marilyn Monroe candlestick.
The Yosemite bison magnet.
The badminton racket bent like a busted nose.
A book of Michelangelo and his Sistine Chapel—
a masterpiece trapped in plaster. Strangers
give us money, and usually, it's women.
They way they do it, though,
drop coins in the curves of our palms,
snatch their hands away as if to avoid the fire
of our fingers. Something about touching us,
they don't like, but something about watching,
they do. We're the ones young women watch for
when they're jogging with their iPods.
We're the men who bathe in rivers, beneath the branches
of summer green. We lie naked on the riverbank,
on a flattened patch of mud. One day I let
a woman watch me, sweaty from her run.
My back against the body of a hard and fallen tree.

The river lapped against my balls, the quiet clap
between my knees. Coils of dark hair wriggled
in the ebb of the river. I let her eyes touch me,
the brown of them, like two fingers dirty with earth.
Being noticed is like being made: Adam
brought to life at the touch of God's knobby finger,
God who strains to reach him from the carriage
of a severed brain. So I didn't flinch, didn't
cup my hands between my legs. I let her
eyes look over me the way water attracts to water.
And with my finger, I will sign my name
in the river, a name she will never know to read.

Pappy

He is a man on all sidewalks,
barely stitched together,
this nomadic cadaver,
this unfastened rag doll,
strung by a single,
flimsy string, shifting
in each turn of the wind.

And the wind turned him
in this direction
on his wayfaring trek
to redemption,
to pause on the sidewalk
he woke from this day,
to hold his cardboard plea
like stone slabs,
like cold concrete paths,
a refugee prophet
sidewalking in the rain.

I wonder at the giving
of good graces
when each day he greets me
through his missing teeth,

that I should have lifted my head
from a pillow today. And when I rest,
not now but forever,
a stone will remember my life,
my days, my name,
while all this man will have

is a sign whose wind-creased plea
will run in Oregon rain.

For now, this is his lot,
this his portion:
walking north and south
on three small slabs
of stone and back again until
the wind calls him a new way,

carrying his bleeding prayer
on a square, the face of a box
that once closed like a tomb
of darkness, of disbelief, despair,

on the back of which I would write
Do Not Disturb
and place outside the rock
I do not roll back.

Urban Legend

"It's best you get yourself out of here, young lady.
You can't be sitting up in here being lost. You know the story."

Pulled over at the side of a city street,
one wrong turn and suddenly I'm in
the part of town where headlines read:
One Found Dead. The part of town

the legends say young women should be scared
to be: being a woman, being young.
I spread the state map over the emblem centered
on my steering wheel, fingers scanning

for the street blocks around my idling car.
The legend on the lower left curls
against my elbow. Because of this key,
I know which roads are interstates,

which roads have tolls; I know where I can
camp for the night or ride a scenic byway.
But I can't tell which streets to avoid
or even find the one I'm on; the legend

doesn't give such streets a marker of their own.
There are no symbols for the corners
where two parents slap each other in the face, child
pinned to her mother's hip, wailing.

There are no symbols for the dumpsters
where people live, the abandoned cars

crammed with boxes, plastic bags
and blankets, or for the basketball courts

where young boys dare each other into cockfights
until they make each other cry. But by this map,
I can identify the university on the east side
of town, where hillside houses rise

like an imagined city street-kids spy on
from their fire escapes in the peal of night's
sirens. Light shines there as it does
not here, where my finger is, where one inch

equals a mile, where my instinct is fear—
a ghost materializing in my rearview
after I say, *It is wrong to be afraid* three times,
though the click of my door lock says I am.

As the story goes, there are strangers outside lurking
and ready to hurt me. My womanhood,
my clean fingernails, my unbroken rows of teeth,
my clothes, the emblem in the center

of my steering wheel—these are the symbols
they look for. A woman, no one
is afraid of me. No one fears the beat of my footsteps
behind them at night, or wonders

what I am doing in my car other than that it's clear
I don't belong, that I need to find my way out,
back to where I came from, back to the Promised Land,
which is just an inch from here in any direction.

What I Learned from Birds

was not how to sing, swoop, or fly.

These birds had fallen from a tree in a parking lot near a wall
covered so thick with ivy that if I pressed
up against it, seven years would disappear.

Treasure or tragedy, a moment would decide. Blood bouldered
through my veins, gathered its greater red as I sprinted
for help: my instinct already given its volume.

Mother and I inspected. The nest, no bigger than the bowl
I could make with my hands, had landed up,
a cradle to a small group of birds only moments old.

Next to it, a mother with a fractured skull, her feathers clotted
on the concrete with a blackened glue of blood.
When the wind blew, her wings would catch in it,

as if about to lift. I learned that not all flapping wings could fly.

We took the birds to a box that once closed over my shoes,
lined with rags, leaves, and sticks. The front porch housed
the live scent of their bodies—not quite birds—

but spongy machines. They glowed blue veins and their tiny
one-hundred-beats-per-minute hearts punched against
their paper breasts. After a whole day of studying
them—little hooks the shape of
an inner-ear—

I learned what I looked like in my mother's womb.

Their eyes bulged milky globes, hard to discern open
from unopened, dead eyes from seeing eyes. But after
three straight days and four pairs of dead eyes,

I learned the difference, could sense the second life went out

the way I could pinpoint the very revolution "Mean Mr. Mustard"
became "Polythene Pam" on the record player.
And so I named them. The third one
had wrenched into his silver hammer

by morning and I learned that two can be a great number.

When it was just Polythene left after a single week,

I learned how far one is from two. I learned that seven days
is an eternity because it takes that little
before a bird's wings tell it to fly.

And when I saw Polythene living out of a box again
years later, I did not recognize her.
In trying to study her from across
Jefferson Street,

I learned how years can sharpen a body out of its gender
so she was no longer a woman but vines of ivy leaf and gears
of a gritty machine. Her hair clotted together in soot
and when wind caught in the clumps, it was as if
knotted birds
were lifting
from her ears.

The distance, I learned, between one place and another, just seconds.

One Week After Christmas

Beneath the Jefferson Street Bridge, Eugene, Oregon, 2009

On a patch of grass, once green,
beneath an overpass of sky,
off a ramp of Interstate 105,
three men steady a tree. Dead
at its ends, branches angled
from rest on the side of the road
where it was discovered, then dragged
here to stand. Car after car careens
past this corner, an endless string
of audience. Red light
at ramp's end chokes the road
with cars for this moment,
frozen in a snow globe. Not
kids sleighing, mouths open
in glee; not mothers baking,
fathers praying near a manger;
not a snowman; not a choo-choo train;
but three men standing back
to admire their tree: its branches
looped with Caution tape,
foil fangled for its star.

Part Two

The Indication

"We don't have any evidence that a weapon was used,"
said Detective Jeff Donaca. "The indication
is that [Herbert Bishop] was beaten to death."

—KVAL.com, June 17th, 2009

The next morning, we went out for breakfast.
Any other Sunday: eggs, sausage, and buttered bread
to sop the beer from last night before it sinks in,
what we did. We washed our hands in the river.
Red blood streamed Willamette green, but you can't see
color in the dark, can't see your reflection either.
The waitress snapped her gum, stared at my knuckles,
cut and dried in blood. Last night, blood throbbed
in my head, greased the machine of me,
as my windmill fists smashed head and chest,

then head
and head
and head.

She stared, but took our order instead:
eggs, sausage, and buttered bread.
The bridge of a nose crushes like a Styrofoam cup,
but the ribs don't give, and the skull is soft like a stone
is soft till finally, the bleeding. All it takes for egg yolk to break
is a toasted crust of bread. Yellow fans out like blood

in the brain from blow after blow after blow. Yolk-thick,
his tongue twitched with slugs of blood. Black like the river
was black, like my coffee is black, like the night was black
before dawn was red and we were a Sunday-kind-
of-hungry, craving some eggs. We stuffed our stomachs
like the pipe we took off him. We went back to get it,
packed it, pulled and held our purple breaths, let them go
like ghosts from our throats, the way life goes out,
but we didn't stay to watch. Couldn't watch that part.
Something wrong about that, the way jerking off feels
wrong the first time you do it till it doesn't anymore.

Reasons

"What strikes me about this case is the senselessness of it," said prosecutor Erik Hasselman. "Usually there is a reason, however weak."

—KVAL.com, January 7th, 2010

I hit because I'm bored,
I'm high,
I'm drunk,

because I'm twenty-three,
because I have
hot blood
and a hairy chin.

I hit because
I can, because
the old man
can't hit back.

I hit because
I suck at math
and because I can
barely read.

Because nobody
ever liked me.

Because my father didn't
teach me not to hit,

or because he hit me
on more than one
occasion. Because

the music I love
is angry. I hit
to smell blood,
to hear an old man cry,
to watch his skin split.

I hit because I want
one less of them
on the streets. Because

I didn't kill enough
tadpoles as a kid. Because
I need to feel
something as good

as my cock
in my hand.

And at least
I didn't hit
a woman.

Under the Blows

"Fifty-six-year-old Herbert Bishop, who did not have a permanent address, was known on the streets as 'Pac-Man.' An autopsy determined yesterday that Bishop died as a result of blunt force trauma."

—*The Oregonion*, May 13th, 2009

When you suffer the first punch,
the prayer you hope others say for you

dips its ladle into your marrow,
pulls it up, your adrenaline stirred.

Before your death's official, though,
you look heavenward for a way home.

But there are two of them—you are all
alone—and defeat descends in your bones

like tree rings. Blow after blow, you lower
to your knees, remember your Genesis,

the man before the fall. You name your every wrong.
You imagine the dimensions of paradise,
and weep for the milk of your mother's breast.

After the boys have left you, you bow your head,
search your blood for a way to put it back.

PSALMS OF THE DINING ROOM

You become a connoisseur of those wounds.
Your features wane at dawn beneath the breath

of a kitten sniffing you, a comfort like the sheet
the police are ready to pull over you. The last sounds

you ever hear are a bell, the flash of a camera,
and a stranger mispronounce your name.

Pac-Man

"[Prosecutor Erik Hasselman] said the two, who shared a nearby apartment, apparently found Bishop sleeping beneath a tree, then kicked and beat him so severely that Bishop suffered twenty-three separate rib fractures and bleeding in his brain. His nose and an eye socket were also broken, and his ears were torn and bleeding."

—*The Register Guard*, December 23RD, 2009

The next morning, a group of Blues bent over me,
flashed light into my eyes, held two rubbered fingers to my neck.
It was morning when they found me in the park.
Sure don't know what I could've looked like laying there—
blood glued to my lips and eyes, my face black from soot
and scab, smashed so I'm a mess that don't look like me no more:
Pac-Man, a man nobody ever knew before.

Maybe the papers'll say I was a good man, maybe even wise.
Maybe the papers'll say everybody liked me.
The papers'll tell the world I didn't fight
back which only egged them on. I could feel
my face change shape, the bottom of a riverbed.

Their hands were wet and clean when they came back.
One pinched my wrist and I shook and twitched,
but they didn't stay. Such a shame to be left like that—
left a bloody mess like that—the way not having
a home feels like a shame till it doesn't anymore.

Justice

The next morning, they went out for breakfast
as if it were any other Sunday—eggs, sausage, buttered bread—
while their victim's wounds gummed with blood,
clogged the machine of his lungs until he choked his last breath.
They washed their hands when they were done, red blood
streamed Willamette green with the stipulated facts
that they had no motive for attack except that their hearts
were black, their blood was black, like the night was black.

No more.

After thirty-two years, I'll hang up my cloak.
I've done my job because justice was served—
twenty-five years for clipping fifty-six years
to minutes or so—but they don't know,
those boys didn't wait for that.

On this stand, justice prevails

and shouldn't it feel good to do justice?
Yes, it feels good to do justice until it doesn't anymore.

The Perpetrators' Guide to Thrill Killing: Lesson One: Practice on a Kitten

"[Herbert] Bishop was one of three local homeless men to die violently in Eugene this year. Gerald Francis Wudarski, 53, died from bleeding inside his brain after a west Eugene man chased and assaulted him . . . James Pelfrey, 36, died in an August 25th stabbing near Eugene's Washington-Jefferson Park . . . In another serious assault, a homeless man was set afire October 3rd as he walked on East Broadway near High Street."

—*The Register Guard*, December 23rd, 2009

First, be a boy always too big for six:
too tall, too loud, too wide.

Wear out words like *asshole*, *prick*,
and *dickhead*, make your daddy proud.

Know what his beer tastes like.

Stink like cigarettes and sweat rings.

When you don't get your way, say

> *Don't be such a scaredy-cat*. What he said to me
> when we were boys, six, with a box of matches
> behind the pool. I watched my neighbor snap
> the stick against the box strip. The flame hissed
> into a slight blast of gold. Before long, it malformed
> into a shattered face, climbed down the stick,
> almost singed his fingertips. He flung it

behind the deck. I shivered, pretended to keep
warm by shaking pool water from my ear.
I tilted my head and hopped on one foot.

Be the first among us to spot her.

Watch her.

Pretend to love her, newly born,
like us, barely furred.

Squat down. Make your shadow small.

Wait for her.

Whisper sweetness as she approaches
your hand, empty of its offering.

Watch her tongue curl against your fist
as if to open it.

Then be quick. Cat-like.

He held the matchstick to me, *Don't be such a scaredy-cat.*
Nearing my face, my neighbor taunted me.
I could feel the pop and purr
of the quivering flame and when I sprinted away,
my blood gunned with dread.
He clapped against me, dragged me
across the gravel drive: my stomach, scraped
and bloody. After a bath of Bactine
and water from the hose, I pulled stones
from my shredded skin, swore I'd never see him again.

Rise.

Shed a heavy darkness.

Hop to your left foot.

Cock your right.

> *Don't be such a scaredy-cat* he said again,
> this time, to his cousin at age thirteen
> because *None of the guns in the house*
> *are loaded*. I couldn't help but shiver.
> I stood there, curious and waiting.

Draw your leg forth to lift and crush
the skull into a shattered blast of light.

Watch, wide-eyed, as blood hurls
through the sky.

Delight.

Watch the corpse crash to the ground.

> Stones come easily when bubbled
> in peroxide, but a boy can't empty bullets
> from his brain the way he shakes water
> from the inner-ear.

Or be a boy too scared to stop it.

The Volunteer

On break from his shift, the Volunteer hunches behind the dumpster.
Matchstick catches and rasps. His skin sizzles gold as he drags
the alley through the V of his fingers. The lanterns tilt
their grim faces; their dim bulbs are the cheekbones of the dead.
Ten minutes are pinched at their tip and flung in the last
mantle of snow, black but still clinging. He treads through
the threshold like tar. His gait grouts the visitors to their places

in the room. If, perhaps his attitude was not *Whatever gets them*
off the streets—because he is sure the homeless,
in their camouflage of grime and wandering,
the homeless in their namelessness can bend themselves
into park benches or roam like dogs, the homeless
can flurry into inexistence like a cloud of ash—then
maybe this morning, only a block away, a man's eyes
would not have been pounded into jelly for feral cats to lick.

This is the last day the Volunteer will be forced to face
the chain-link of faces, men with hands grimed
by the only land they know as home. They inch to the right,
as their plates collect grapes, chicken and potatoes, then fall off
the line to the tables to eat. At five, the Volunteer balls his apron
pitches it at the crate, misses. He scrubs his hands, lobs
a wadded towel over his shoulder. It lands on the lip of the garbage bin

then tips off its edge. The Volunteer thinks this is his last day
at the kitchen, but he will end up here again. He got off too easily
this time: twenty hours of service for a dime-bag in his backpack.
He doesn't know that one day he will torch a man with matches,
blaze three quarters of a thrashing body. He will study
how skin drips from bone like caramel. Then a guilt

so heavy he will lift his back against it just to take his morning piss.
    He will stare at another man's slash-marks knifed on the wall,

grouped in fives like twigs, like unlit matchsticks.
    Today, he does not know how quickly youth will slip off
    his cheekbones, how soon his shoulders will fold. It's in the way
he measures these men in mashed potatoes, the way he snaps them
    from spoon to plate. It's in the clack the spoon makes,
    the way their plates give a little under the weight.
It's in the eyes these men barely lift to greet him.

As I Roll Silverware

In Memory of Herbert "Pac-Man" Bishop

In the quietest hour, before the first meal
is served, I roll the evening's silverware.
Mismatched silverware. Warm and stained
with hard-water silverware.

The rhythm:

Wrap. Roll. Stack it.
Wrap. Roll. Stack it.

Bundled like bodies after the war,
I think of all the names I know,
say each and every name I know.

Wrap. Roll. Stack it.
Wrap. Roll. Stack it.

Lester Ansel. Stanley Wenslow.
Pedro Orpeza. Fanny Anderson.
Jeff Rowberry. Onorio Ortiz.
Edgar Orth. Marilyn Williams.
Melaney and John in the rhythm:

Wrap. Roll. Stack it.
Wrap. Roll. Stack it.

Frank slumps in with a limp, waves,
greets everyone by name. Patty and Bob pray
over their plates. Marge scrapes beets
from her plate onto a hungry stranger's plate.

Wrap. Roll. Stack it.
Wrap. Roll. Stack it.

But there was a name I did not know.
Didn't know his name. Didn't ask it.
Herbert Bishop, papers said. Homeless
male, fifty-three. Third killed this year.
Two boys, twenties, found him
there beneath the Jefferson Street Bridge,
where he lived, beneath the Jefferson Street Bridge,
trying to sleep beneath the bridge.
They didn't know his name. Didn't ask it.

Wrap. Roll. Stack it.
Wrap. Roll. Stack it.

Fist by fist, they thrashed him.
Wanted to know what violence feels like,
to know what the crush of a nose feels like,
the wetness of blood, what a broken bone feels like.

Wrap. Roll. Stack it.
Wrap. Roll. Stack it . . .

In a world far from this, a young boy finds
a bomber's arm, blown through his bedroom
window, from the other side of the street.
He feels the hand with his fingers, throws it
to the fire biting the city street.

PSALMS OF THE DINING ROOM

The boy's sun descends as it rises here,
on this city street. The news of Bishop spreads,
his name is a fire in this city street.

In the quietest hour, before the first meal is served,
I bundle the evening's silverware
and practice all their names.

Her Name is Sarah

When Randy drifted in for dinner with her baby
tangled in the rosary scars of her arms,
pressed against the dust of her breast,
everyone wanted to see. They softened
their eyes, their smiles, the way people do
when they look on a baby sleeping,
a baby who has not cried in two days,
a baby whose eyes ooze a thick glue,
whose lips are latched in a palsied twist.
Her name is Sarah, she whispers, hushing her lips
shut with a finger because her baby is sleeping.
The onlookers looked at her, at each other,
at the baby, away altogether. They cupped
their noses and mouths as the wet stench lifted,
red sirens ringing in the backs of their throats.
The bad-news angel-coat slung the stethoscope
over his shoulder, pulled rubber from his hands,
scrubbed to his elbows, left with a black bag.

Today, Randy drifts in for dinner with her baby:
plastic-happy and blue-eyed, perfect smile,
a baby that never cries. *Her name is Sarah*,
she says, and no one calls the authorities.

Elimination Half-Life

Four things. All a body wants. Four things.
    Food. Drink. Sex. Sleep.
In no particular order, sometimes all

    at once. A circuit of strings
pulls in and out over the body's systematic wheel,
    tugs up buckets from the well
of when and what the body wants:

    the sweet glaze of butter on a tongue;
the crisp sip of wine; the jab of pleasure between
    the legs where generations lodge until called;
dreams like a soft animal that dies upon waking.

    The cool blade of darkness strikes
open the folds wherein hide the body's
    authentic splendors. April has arrived
and the day is given back the light we're owed

    at the end of four o'clock in winter.
Where has that light been but some rehab room
    with inconvenient visiting hours? Today,
we unclose our eyes where meth has made its bed.

    The noonday will feed our blood a meal of sun,
a gulp of blue-sky April rain. Addiction thins.
    The Resurrection does not happen
once but always here, because the past is chemical-
    drenched, shoved in a refrigerator drawer

keeping it fresh, until. Soon we'll plunge
our minds in formaldehyde, or chill them on ice,
maybe plant them in soil, or restore them

to their systems. Only in a solar eclipse
can Earth see Mercury. Perhaps twelve years
is too long for addiction to cast its dark radius,
but measure me the circumference of sun-shot

and we can do the math. Smallest planet, too near
to the glare, condemned to dusk if only by comparison.
In dreams we catch glimpses of all we will never
get to be— the flash of horses on a snow-stroked horizon.

Our eyes dull until the only light left in the face
is the dim flicker of the television, halving the price
of knives to two easy payments of $19.95.
In the morning, the body discovers some fifth thing,

having lasted through the night.

Part Three

The Milk Rule

As I reach over
a man to give him
one small cup of milk,

he grabs me
just above the elbow,
just below the wrist,
slips his drug-black gums
around my forearm.
A harmless beast
pretending to eat,
he snarls at my skin,
slimes me with a mixture
of spit and scraps
of half-chewed,
broiled meat.

He howls with delight
after his feast—happy
he could make me laugh,
even though I spilled
his only cup of milk.

Junk Mail Meditation

Every day is the day of the luckless at this kitchen, and hope
is a side-dish to steak on Mondays. The potatoes
of a second chance. Sorry, folks, one helping only.
Barely enough for everyone and the reason
the community leaves canned goods out for the mailman
to collect each November. Why couldn't hope be doled out
like junk mail? So much daily overflow, there are receptacles
for discard. Why Pizza Hut seems to think I need
three leaflets of coupons a week, why Comcast
wants to hook me up with better options, why Visa
keeps offering me its approval—these are worth
asking. I'm on a list with my address and if I ever move,
I will be found, no doubt, though my apartment's previous
resident can still collect her junk mail here on occasion.
Junk mail misfires. Statements, surveys, leaflets,
flyers, pamphlets, catalogues, postcards, newsletters,
announcements, special deals, free trial memberships, savings,
a subscription to *Vogue* I've neither read nor paid for.
All these pile in my apartment like prayers
I slosh around in until I take my trash out.
Junk mail stacked on the dinette set, junk mail on the floor.
Coffee table strewn with junk mail, junk mail filed away.
A desk trapped under junk mail. Soon, a toilet flushing
junk mail, bathtub flooding junk mail. Then cupboards stuffed
with junk mail. Sandwich: turkey, cheese and junk mail . . .

I've been told to shred mail with my name on it,
so no one sifting through my scraps can learn anything
valuable about me: my name, date of birth, papers
that prove I exist. But it doesn't matter. The junk mail centers
know where I live: they keep sending me their coupons.

My mother used to clip coupons on Sundays,
to make more of little on the limited time offers,
that dash between the date of use and expiration.
I come here to learn to do the same thing. To see
how a little goes a long way and not the other way
around, as Visa would have me believe. Because
when the visitors look at me, they see how little
a long way is from where they are, because it's here,
serving them the nutrition of eye contact and a smile.
They make room in themselves for whatever they need
for wholeness. Some chug the last gulp of their only cup of milk
so I don't have to make a second trip. Some drop their forks
in the busser's bin so I don't have to strain. Some wipe the mess
they've made, or linger over tea. They are never without
their *Thank Yous*, or a *How you doin', girl?*
They are never without and never ask for seconds, never more
than what they're given which is always enough,
I must remember, when I'm neck-high in my junk mail.

Far from Butter

I scrub my hands clean three times.
Anti-septic soap stings my fingers;
its stink burns my eyes and they water.

I stand behind the waist-high table
in the kitchen with offerings of butter,
half-frozen sticks of must-be-used today

butter, stacked sticks of unfit-for-sale butter.
This evening, I must cut them into even pats,
each the width of a nickel, one pat per visitor.

The butter is so cold that I must lean
my weight on the spine of a meat cleaver
to force the blade through until it touches

the table. A deep ridge forms across my palms
like a lash mark. Looking at my hands,
pink and swollen, it is clear that I lack the strength

to cut through this wealth of refrigerated butter,
much less the strength to make it. I lack the patience
to wait for milk and cream to pull their bodies

apart from their emulsive embrace so the cream
can rest on top. I lack the precision it takes
to skim that thick collection at the hem where

cream and milk meet. My forearms are too slight
to press into the belly of that wad of fat
for it to release its milk. I don't have the shoulders

to churn that butter, or the hands to give it its texture.
            It is only in feeling a bar begin to melt beneath
my warm grip, like a muscle grown weak,

that I realize how far I am from butter, the work
it takes to make that butter. The kind of work
            that is holy like butter. Not water-into-wine work,
but real work, hard work, work we can be grateful exists

if for no other reason than the joy that comes
            when it's done. I want to taste that holiness,
so I pull a pat of nickel-thick butter stuck to the flat edge

of the blade and drop it on my tongue.
I push it to the roof of my mouth at the seam
            of teeth and gum, and wait for it to melt
to tell me that I know nothing of how to suffer.

Manny

For Manny

Manny got a job today. After nine months
of pushing peas around his plate, eyes he could not
bear to lift, Manny got a job today. Then this could be

the day the burns on Berta's arm iron out
and tighten, the day her butterfly fingers separate
from the cocoon of cells that swathes them. This could be
the day she pulls her shirt over her shoulder,
lengthens her limb through the sleeve with ease,
extends the crook, fused in a melted web of skin,
so she no longer smuggles her arm in the belly
of her shirt as if to soothe an ache. This could be

the day the rot in Rico's leg dries its vast jungle,
the day the claw of red ripped skin releases its grip
in the heart-shaped carve of his calf, the day
his cane is used for dancing. This could be

the day the scourge of sores on Salena's lips
seal shut, the day the yellow-green scabs flake away
and her moldy breath sweetens. This could be

the day the fear coiled in Doyle's mind lifts
like smoke rings and fades, the day he forgets
his wife's bones he put above a fire. This could be

the day Jay's machine-gun gibberish becomes prayer
or poetry, praise, or warning, the day the tank in his throat
cranks its belts into the soft pulses of a baritone,
the day he learns to sing. This could be

the day the scar that halves Marva's face unzips,
the day her albino eye flushes its gray and glimmers,
warm with brown and sight again, the day the right side
of her face sits on the throne of her skull, the day
the Z in her spine straightens. This could be

the day the spectacle of Kenneth's gender is quelled,
the day she learns to carry asymmetric breasts
and pack away her penis, the day God is merciful
and stuffs him into the purse of a body he was not
born into but wears around his shoulder. This could be

the day everyone lifts their glasses. Manny got a job today.
The day silver stays in drawers and napkins folded away.
The day there's more than enough for seconds. Manny got a job today.
The day the doors are boarded up, the day the *Closed* sign is hung.
Manny got a job today. Yes, Manny got a job today.

Kenneth's Purse

Not a woman's purse, but a little girl's purse:
sequined and pink, the strap barely enough
for Kenneth to fit her arm through.
She wears a teenager's T-shirt,
baby blue and too small to hide
the roll of belly, the fur that coils
down to the groin, or the bra straps.

I do not wonder if that hair bothers her,
if she feels about it the way I feel
about my thighs. I do not wonder
what's beneath her jeans, if she throbs
seeing a naked woman or man; I do not wonder
about her breasts, if they're real or if
they're a balled pair of socks, why they're lopsided
and uneven. I do not wonder if she must shave
her face twice a day, or if it's Secret or Old Spice
behind her bathroom mirror. I am not curious
about the voice she is careful not to use.

But I do wonder what's inside that purse.

Maybe she carries the cold hands she used to wear
in the days she spent digging for stones
along the coast in a forest of Douglas fir.
Maybe a familiar voice calling her home for dinner,
or all the lima beans she never ate.
Maybe she's kept the gutted deer she found dangling
from a neighbor's tree, or the flies that bounced around
in the strips of shredded flesh. Maybe she carries
the raccoons that cackled in the backyard shed

and gave her nightmares all her life. Or the punch
her brother left in her stomach when she embarrassed
him before his friends. Maybe she carries a moonlit kiss,
or a Christmas ornament, the first word she ever spoke.
Maybe she keeps music in there: love songs, or songs
of dreams and journeys. And laughter. How I hope
there is some laughter. Maybe she carries all
the advice she never took about baseball, love,
or how to defend herself against the sideways glances
that began in seventh grade, the whispers, the lookers
who tried not to look, or the ones who looked
like they were trying not to look. Maybe she keeps
the word *Faggot* in that purse, or *Queer, Freak, Pussy,*
Homo. Maybe she keeps the written notes, the threats,
the eating alone at lunchtime, the long walk home
from school. Maybe she keeps the prayer she says
to herself, or the tampon she wishes she could use.

I don't know what's inside that purse, but today I saw
something to be added: the warmth left on the seat
across the table from her where a man sat down
and asked her to say her name, the name
she gave herself, the way a bird must name herself
the first time she bursts from trees to flight.

Dining with Dignity

It was a smell I'd smelled
only once before—a gas station
port-a-john stuffed so full
of shit and piss, the heap
crowned the toilet seat—
but this was a human being.
His scent swung its blades
through the room, slicing
into people who refused
to let on, the busboy, most
especially, who waited for the man
to leave, then tilted the chair
on its two front legs to close
that corner table for cleaning.

The Coffee Station

For John

Behind the counter, I rag away rings of brew, dab
drips of cream, stick teaspoons in a tin cylinder.
I replenish the sugar, replace the mugs as they go
missing, refill pitchers before they drain. The sounds
of mealtime fall in the room like frosty light, rest
on shoulders, cheeks, and noses. Chatter hums inside
the colors of the mural, the size of the entire wall
behind me. It's as if I stand inside the painting as I stand
inside this room, this room that is the painting.

You tiptoe to the bar. The palm of your hand is chapped
and red, raw like a split fish as you reach for a mug.
You pull from the center of the tray, always from the center
of the tray. Today, *World's Greatest Grandpa* hugs the cup,
the phrase scrawled in a crayoned font, a backwards N
as if your granddaughter were the one who wrote it.
I greet you. You grin, nod and say nothing. Though charmed
by the various silences we always seem to manage, the moment
clanks away: forks scrape dishes, plastic cups clunk
when dropped into the busser's bin. The clamor would drown

your quiet voice, assuming that you had one. Once
our fingers touched, both of us reaching for the mugs.
You snatched your arm away as if the brush of my skin
had burned you. I said I was sorry, racked the mugs
with my hands, replaced the rows from behind.

PSALMS OF THE DINING ROOM

Today will be the last day I ever see you. I know this
because you said so, though not at first. First, you poured
your coffee, brimmed with something akin to shame. The pause
between us was an abandoned stairwell where pigeons swoop
and coo. You shuffled away, eyes quivering in your cup.
Warm from the river of brew bubbling deeply in your gut,
you returned to speak your only words to me—
something of the way I look at you—and a new silence bloomed.
You gave yourself a name, John, you told me where you'll go,
but tomorrow I will stand here, this same mural at my back,
and I will listen for your voice. I will listen for your voice.

Marlon's Fingers

Still lookin' for 'em, you joked
a year ago, the first time
my eyes locked on your fingers,
the little that's left of them:
ring and index
clipped at the knuckle;
thumb missing part of its tip;
pinky severed altogether.
The middle untouched,
a gesture kept at the ready.

My face lit with shame.
You grinned, blew me a kiss,
extended your hand to shake mine,
but when I reached across the coffee counter,
you waved me off, shook your head,
and winked. You just couldn't
do that to me, make me touch you.
Secretly, I was grateful then,
could feel those fingers tickle my spine.

They gave me that slightly sick feeling
I still get when I look at the portrait
of my grandfather sitting on the sofa.
The photographer peeled open
the claw the stroke made of his hand,
spread his fingers over his bent knee so it appeared
casual, my grandfather relaxed,
just sitting there, hand on his kneecap.
A hand that was there but not there,
always clenched and cool like a lure

at the end a dead arm. When we could not
make out his words, he would spit, curse
or cry, and that arm would tremble
as if a live wire snaked through it.
Fingers would burst open then snap shut,
an exotic plant feasting on insects.

But there, in that picture, it is the hand
that once wielded a trowel to close
weather-made breaks in concrete,
to reinforce a wall so the two sides
touch again. In that picture, it is the hand
that pressed a heads-up penny into the wet slab
of cement outside our backyard shed, a joke
hoping to trick visitors into bending over

to pick it up for luck. I know better
than to pluck at the edges of that penny
in this land, in times like these,
when a poor man can earn a buck by letting
a stranger make trunks of his fingers for fun,
but when you beam at me and say,
Still can't remember where I put 'em.
You been lookin' for 'em, Sweetie?
I am willing to play along, willing
to fall for that trick again:
I pat down my apron pockets,
my pant legs, I lift up a coffee mug
or two, pretend to peer underneath,
I unroll napkin-bundled silverware
to check between the fork and spoon.
Maybe they're floating in the soup? I say.

Such hope, Marlon, in how you rise from the booth,
how you smile at me before you leave,
how you sling your denim coat
over your shoulders, swiftly and one-handed,
how you pinch the copper buttons through the holes
using your thumb and middle finger only.

The Magic Trick of the Table

The Dining Room has just opened and in rolls Stanley,
spokes flickering, the steady gears of his entrance
every day. His pant legs deflate at the knees,
pinned to themselves like two ghosts twisting
in a grimace. Underneath, pain drags a string of razorblades
through the airy sleeve. Stanley thrashes to clasp
his absent, burning calf. Was it war or did it happen
in the mysterious purple universe where he grew
from fluid into human, or a high shed and a dare
before bones blasted through skin, then shattered
into a thousand cries for *mother*? At this table, Stanley
is like any other man. Its glossy top slashes him in half,
makes a phantom of his missing limbs. At this table, Stanley
pounds his heavy fists, sends the plates leaping
with glee at another man's jokes. Here, Stanley
rises from the magic trick of the table, marked like a jester
by the wrinkles that bracket his eyes. Here, he waits
for Brandy to bring him the plate of chicken he divides
with fork and knife while she sits across from him and smiles.
At this table, Stanley imagines muscle braiding slowly
over bone, and the coldness of her toe sliding up his pant leg.

Unwintering

For Jennifer

On the last day of winter I watched a frog
unlock its death in a bed of once-red leaves
flecked with mud and amber shards of light.

It thawed out in one even note,
drummed from its pitchfork the way they do
when they come back in spring: spongy,

soft with life, croaking their songs
which sound almost beautiful.

I thought of you as a child in that house
where you learned to freeze against yourself

so he, your winterer, would leave your quilted leaves
unturned long enough until spring, so maybe
you could come back again. But there are those cracks,

as in ice—sprawled out like fingers on your skin—the scars
you opened all over yourself to release your body's heat.

I thought of you as a child in that bed of tears
and blood divided from your skin, where soon,

a child will divide from you.

You are frozen on the outside, still,
but your cell, your womb, still warm, and waiting.

You will come back to life when you deliver it,
when she is pulled from the bed of your blood-flesh,

spongy, soft with life, croaking her song:
her reminder of your return.

Acquired Tastes (or Sam's Song)

We used to spit out the food our mother gave us:
my brother's face would pinch and twist at broccoli.
Each feature—eyes, cheeks, and lips—on separate springs,
all at once latching and unlocking in spastic labors.
And when mother fed me prunes, Oh the violence!—
my face a fish snagged on a line. I would flop
and buck, my spine rounding in metered humps.
The upchucked plum, the color of chewed placenta,
would congeal on my plate in a thick batch of spit.
A woman now, I eat prunes with ease and brother
shows his daughters how well he tummies his greens.
Such flavors have not changed. Those ropy roots still bleed
bitterness, and the awful purple sack still swells with gall.

I have heard that we don't ever learn to love broccoli,
but that there are fewer buds on our tongue as we age,
that the senses protect us, and that our tolerance of broccoli
and rain is nothing more than a loss at how to feel
the world. In truth, I am grateful for this because lately,
it seems like the trees' caterpillars are stuck
spinning in a single strand of web, and that while the days
of my life should amount to something, I have only
furry-browed blueberries to show. Lately, it seems
like the sum of thirty years has only a single plotline:
boy meets girl, love then marriage, and of course,
the war somewhere. What I wouldn't give
for an alternate ending because lately, it seems
like the sun is passing up the best chances to shine,
that spring is so beautiful, I must postpone my visit there.
Every night I dream only of losing my keys
and I don't know what this means other than that

I need a better system, something to hang them from
on the wall in my kitchen. The other day, I gave an apple
to a man who had not a single tooth in his grin.
And isn't that the only way to say that hope is in a boat
with one oar stronger than the other? Lately, it feels like
brotherhood is a man in a trench coat picking up
stepped-on cigarettes and asking for a light.
It feels like luck doesn't have a permanent
address, that the Get Well cards I keep sending
are received more likely by a tenant who lives there now.
Lately, it feels like empathy is a glacial pool I wish

I could do more than sink my toe in. But when I hear you
play your song, Sam, with your blue-grey Fender
and your one-man amp, I feel like I can bear this kitchen,
these rain-slick streets, I can even stand *The New York Times*,
so I've tucked that song in the lapel pockets of my ears,
and every morning I will find it again as I'm looking for my keys.

Prayer

For Jeremy

When I clear your table after you've gone, there's a small scrap
of paper which reads: "God Bless You. You are Beautiful.
I Promise to Pray for You." *Pray* for me? Pray for *me?*
Then pray for me that I wake up in the morning in a bed
and lie there, that I give my blessings their proper names
and faces, the blessings that keep me from a life too like
yours, pray for me. Because the first thought of my day

is hunger, pray for me that I eat. But pray for me that I know
hunger, pray for me. Pray for me that I feel myself in
the growl of your belly, that I remember I am more like you
than I remember, pray for me. Pray for me that I am Rodney
with his weary eyes who is all at once teacher, cousin,
neighbor, friend, and the stranger who held the door for me
when my arms were full of bags, please pray. Pray for me

that I am the woman with earth-rich skin. Pray for those hands
that slammed her plate face-down into the table for me to clean.
Pray for me that I know no such grief, pray for me.
Pray for me that I am Larry whose fingers shoot music
into the belly of the piano; those same seven songs spark
from its upright head. Pray for me that I have the comfort
of knowing what comes next, pray for me. Pray for me that I am
the blind man because the room knows to make room for him.
People move tables, chairs, themselves, part a path for him as if
he were a king. But pray for me that I make way, pray for me.

Pray for me that I am Amber with her Vaseline face,
whose words are frenzied centipedes that scatter from her lips
and braid above her head. She stares at them like a mobile
or a noose. She stares at them like she would a heaven. Pray for me

there's a heaven. That the demons inked along Leanne's spine
do not exist, pray for me. Pray for me that my back can carry
such blackness if it needs to, pray for me. Pray for me that I am
the pregnant girl who is allowed a second plate. Pray that I know
the power I hold in my body, for a tiny king can grow eyes

in my body, please pray. Pray for me that I am the man
in this same room, seated at another table, the man
that gives the girl his milk. Pray for me that I remember
to give up my milk. Pray for me that I am the milk.

20982249R00050

Made in the USA
Middletown, DE
11 December 2018